A New True Book

THE ESKIMO
THE INUIT AND YUPIK PEOPLE

By Alice Osinski

*The author would like to thank
Linda J. Ellanna, Ph.D., University of
Alaska, Juneau, for her assistance.*

CHILDRENS PRESS ®

CHICAGO

A hunter searches along the ice for seals.

Library of Congress Cataloging in Publication Data

Osinski, Alice.
The Eskimo.

(A New true book)
Includes index.
Summary: Describes the natural environment and traditional way of life of the Eskimos, contrasting their old customs with the new lifestyle brought by modern civilization.
1. Eskimos—Juvenile literature. [1. Eskimos I. Title.
E99.E70782 1985 979.8'00497 85-9691
ISBN 0-516-01267-3

TABLE OF CONTENTS

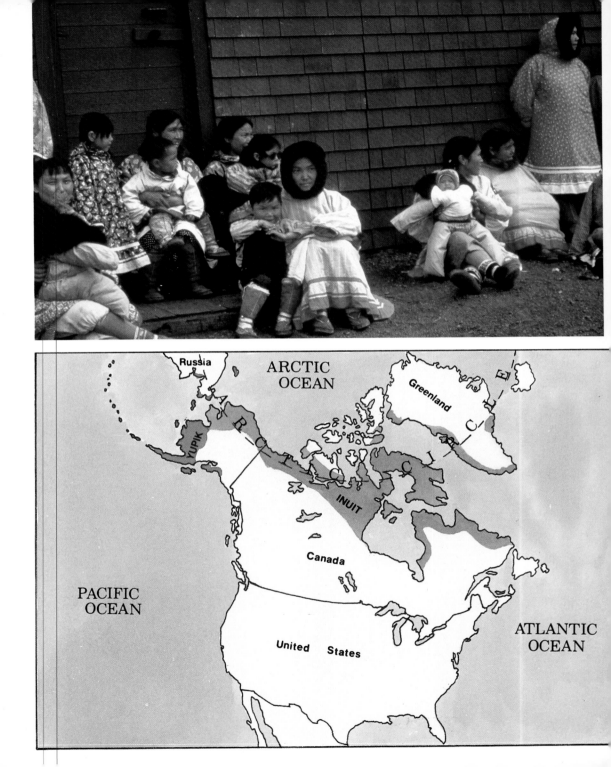

PEOPLE OF THE FAR NORTH

At the northern tip of the earth lies a land of snow and ice. It is the Arctic. South of the Arctic is a region called the subarctic.

Two special groups of people live on this land that stretches from Russia to Greenland, across Alaska and Canada. They call themselves Inuits and Yupiks, "the real people." We know them as Eskimo.

A LAND OF FROZEN BEAUTY

Inuit and Yupik people live in one of the coldest but most beautiful regions of the world. They have learned to live with the cold—whether on the snow-covered plains in the north, on the grasslands or in the forests of the south,

Snow covers the land most of the year in the Arctic, although it snows only a few times.

or inland from the coast.

For those who live in the Arctic, cold is a constant companion. Except for three months of the year, the land remains frozen.

Spring arrives late. Snowfall still occurs in March and April. By May and June the snow melts. For three months the land becomes a swamp of freshly melted streams,

Mouselike lemmings (left) and caribou (above)
spend the summer in the Arctic.

grass, moss, berries, and
wildflowers. Herds of
hungry caribou, musk-oxen,
and tiny lemmings return
to feed off the berries and
moss. Many kinds of

Horned puffins (left) live in the Arctic waters.
Walrus (right) rest along the shores in summer.

birds come back. The sea
is alive with seals, walrus,
and whales. Salmon return
in spring and summer.

Musk-oxen have curved hooves to help them travel easily.

July and August are the summer months in the Arctic. The temperature often does not get warmer than 50 degrees Fahrenheit. By the middle of September light snow begins to fall again.

By October the first heavy snowfalls begin. All living things prepare for the coming winter, when temperatures can fall to 50 degrees below zero.

The arctic fox (below) and the willow ptarmigan (right) grow new white coats for winter.

HUNTING FROM SEASON TO SEASON

To survive in the cold climate, Inuits and Yupiks depended on animals. They hunted animals for food and dressed in animal skins. They followed the animals from season to season.

A hunter harpoons a bearded seal.

They learned to trap, hunt, and gather everything that could be eaten or used.

Most people lived along the coast and hunted seals year-round. In winter and spring they hunted seals on foot. In summer and early fall, seals were hunted from small boats.

Hunting seals in winter took the most patience. Seals live below the ice in winter. When they need air, they swim to a breathing hole they have made in the ice. A hunter may wait many hours, or even days, before a seal comes to the hole where he waits. When a seal appears, the hunter has to harpoon the seal before it goes

Walrus-skin rope (left) is twenty times stronger than regular rope.

below the ice again.

In the past, most of what Inuits and Yupiks needed came from the seal, caribou, salmon, and walrus: meat; skins and bones for clothing, tents, boats, and tools; and oil for heat and light.

A Yupik woman dries salmon for the winter.

Whales were hunted along the coast in spring and summer. People hunted caribou also. They hunted seabirds and collected bird eggs. Along rivers they trapped or netted fish such as salmon, char, and trout.

CROSSING LAND AND SEA

Like all hunters, Inuits and Yupiks traveled year-round to find food. To make travel easier, they built boats and dogsleds.

Dogs carried backpacks during summer hunts and pulled sleds in winter and spring. Sleds were made of bone or wood slats sometimes tied together with animal skin.

Wood is scarce in the Arctic. When driftwood is found, it is often carried long distances.

Today some families still use dog teams for travel. Four to twelve huskies make up a team. The front dog, called the lead dog, listens carefully for directions and then leads the other dogs.

Hunters in kayaks, 1925

Boats were an important
means of travel in spring
and summer. Two types of
boats were used: kayaks
and umiaks. The kayak
was small. It carried
one or two people.
It had a wooden frame
covered with seal or

A modern kayak

caribou skin. A hunter
usually wore a waterproof
jacket when riding in a
kayak. The jacket was
attached to the boat. It
sealed the rider in the
boat and kept him afloat
if the kayak rolled over.

Modern umiaks often have outboard motors.

The umiak was a large, open boat. It could carry more than ten people. It was made of bearded seal or walrus skin stretched and sewn together over a wooden frame. It was used for long trips or to hunt large sea animals.

SUMMER AND WINTER HOMES

Only the Inuits and Yupiks who lived in Alaska usually built permanent homes. The others lived in sod or skin shelters that could be quickly and easily made. They built their houses strong enough to withstand bad weather.

Most families had summer and winter homes.

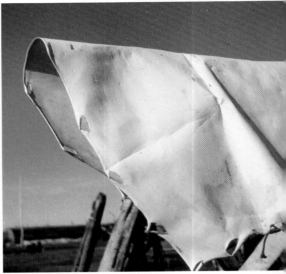

In the past, sealskins were sewn together to make tents. Today some families live in canvas tents during the summer.

During the summer some people lived in tents. Women made the tents by sewing the skins of caribou or seals together. They stretched the skins over driftwood, or over whale, seal, or walrus bones.

A sod house

In winter families built sod houses or snow houses called igloos. Sod houses were made of soil and were built partly underground. Often they were used for more than one winter.

Snow houses were made
of blocks of hard-packed
snow. Usually snow houses
were built on ice where
hunting was good. Two
men, working quickly,
could build an igloo in two
hours. Sometimes skins,

used for the family tent in summer, were hung inside the igloo to help keep out the cold. A lamp, carved from a soft stone called soapstone, was placed in the center of the igloo for warmth and light.

Sometimes several families camped together at winter hunting grounds. They joined igloos together with tunnels so they could visit one another without going outdoors.

KEEPING WARM

Both Inuit and Yupik women made clothing from caribou skin. It was the best kind of animal skin for cold climates. It was warm and light. Skins of seals, polar bears, squirrels, and arctic foxes were used, too.

Everyone wore a hooded jacket called a parka. They also wore pants, socks, mittens, and boots. Tiny skin boots were even put

Caribou skin (left) was dried in the fall. It took almost twelve skins to make a set of winter clothes for an adult.

on dogs' paws to protect them from the sharp ice in spring.

In colder regions people wore two jackets. The inner jacket had fur

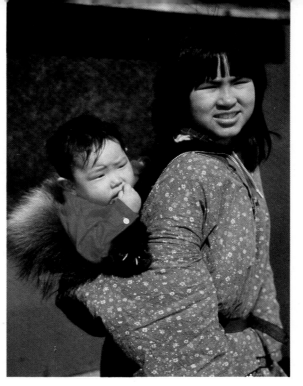

Children learned tasks at an early age. Girls were taught to prepare food, make clothing, and care for babies. Boys learned to hunt and to build igloos.

next to the skin for warmth and softness. The outer jacket had fur on the outside. Clothing was loose fitting. It trapped warm air between the body and the cold air outside. A woman's parka had extra

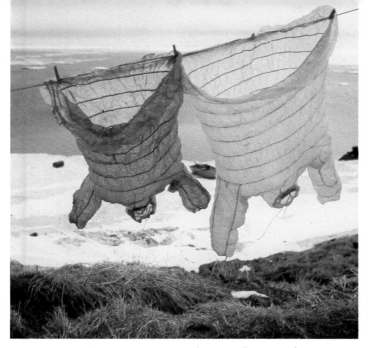

In some areas raincoats are still made from the intestines of seals.

room in the back so a baby could be carried against her warm body. In summer people usually wore only a rainproof suit made of seal intestines.

Women made all the clothing by hand. Many hours were spent fixing

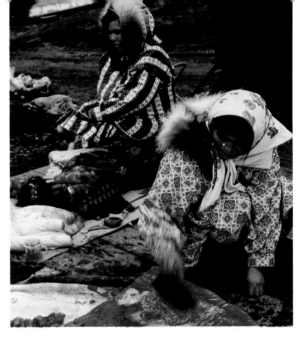

Women learned to sew in childhood. When they married, they took with them their bone knives, used for scraping hides, and their sewing kits.

worn clothes and preparing skins for new clothing. Women took special care of their husbands' clothing. They dried the clothes each night. In the morning, if the men's boots were hard, the women chewed them to soften the hide.

ART AND STORYTELLING

Inuit and Yupik families spent much of the long winter months inside their homes. They made things they would need for hunting and cooking during the year. They also played games and told stories called legends.

Some people made beautiful carvings of the animals they hunted. In Canada most carvings were made from soapstone. In Alaska bone and ivory were used. Carving was a special art. Not just any stone was used. An artist spent time holding a stone and thinking about it before carving it.

Men weave baskets of baleen (whalebone) and carve animals from ivory. Some still use the ancient bow drill (bottom left). Soapstone (bottom right) has a soft soapy feeling.

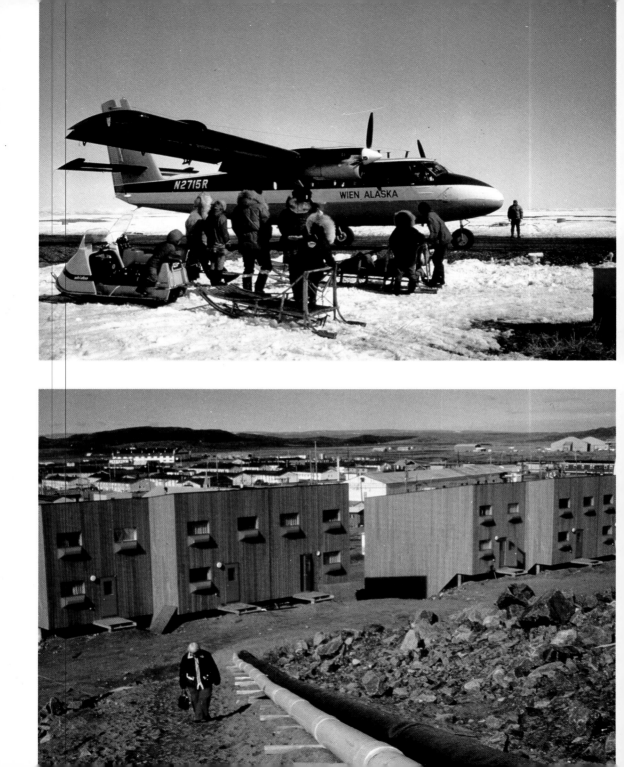

MODERN LIFE

Life is somewhat different for Inuits and Yupiks today. Although they still depend on the land and animals for their way of life, there have been many changes.

Hospitals, schools, airstrips, and stores provide for many of their needs. Modern houses have taken the place of sod houses and igloos.

Electric lights and stoves do the work of soapstone lamps. In many areas snowmobiles, airplanes, and motorboats have replaced dogsleds, kayaks, and umiaks. Skin clothing is not usually worn. Some of the animals people once hunted are now rare or endangered. It is against the law to hunt them in great numbers.

But progress has created many problems for people and for animals. Highways and pipelines built by oil companies have been changing the countryside and disturbing the animals on which people depend.

The Trans-Alaskan pipeline

Boots called mukluks
are still made with a bearded
sealskin sole. The style has
changed little over the
past 1,000 years.

Inuits and Yupiks like
modern ways, but they want
to hold on to their old ways,
too. They are proud of
their customs. Many
depend on hunting, fishing,
trapping, and gathering for
their way of life.

After a whale has
been killed, people
gather (above) to
honor the hunters
and the spirit
of the whale,
and share what
they have caught.
The blanket
toss (right) was
an old Inuit
custom to help
hunters find animals.

Native dance is a form of storytelling—told mainly by hand and arm motions. These children (above) have learned the dance of the seal hunt.

At special times everyone comes together to sing, to dance, and to share their legends.

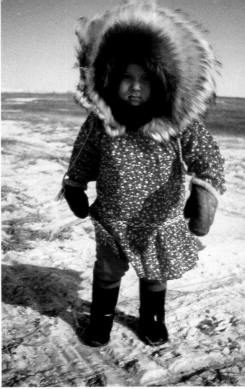

Schools prepare children for the future.
Some will become the next Inuit and
Yupik teachers and leaders.

Today Inuits and Yupiks
use modern tools and modern
transportation. Although new
industries are being
created to provide jobs for
people in villages, living
off the land continues to
be very important to the
Inuit and Yupik way of life.

WORDS YOU SHOULD KNOW

afloat(uh • FLOHT) — floating; on the sea

Arctic(ARK • tik) — the region at the northern tip of the globe, near the North Pole

carving(KAR • ving) — cutting away wood, stone, or some other material to make a shape of some kind

climate(KLY • mit) — the usual type of weather in a certain place

coast(KOHST) — land near a shore

custom(KUHS • tum) — a practice common to one group of people

endangered(en • DAYN • jerd) — in danger of dying out

harpoon(har • POON) — a long spear with a line attached, used to catch fish, seals, and whales

husky(HUHSS • kee) — a dog with a heavy coat that lives in the Arctic

igloo(IG • loo) — a house made of blocks of snow

industry(IN • dus • tree) — business

inland(IN • land) — away from the sea

Inuit(IN • oo • it) — Eskimo people who live from northwestern Alaska, across Canada, into Greenland, and speak the Inupiaq language

ivory(EYE • vree) — the material that makes up the tusks of walrus and elephants

kayak(KYE • ak) — a small boat for one or two people, made of skins stretched over a wooden frame

legend(LEJ • und) — a story that has come down from the past

moss(MAWSS) — a type of tiny plant that grows in moist or swampy places

parka(PAR • kuh) — a fur jacket with a hood, worn in the Arctic
pipeline(PYE • pline) — a long line of pipe for moving liquids or gases
progress(PRAHG • res) — movement toward a more advanced stage
soapstone(SOHP • stohn) — a soft stone that is easy to carve
sod house(SAHD HOWSS) — a house made of sod, or blocks of soil held together by plant roots
subarctic(sub • ARK • tik) — land directly south of the Arctic
survive(ser • VYVE) — to continue to live
swamp(SWAMP) — land that is wet and often covered with water
temperature(TEM • per • uh • cher) — the degree of hotness or coldness of something, as measured by a thermometer
umiak(OO • mee • ak) — a large boat, for ten or more people, made of skins stretched over a wooden frame
waterproof(waht • er • PROOF) — able to keep out water
Yupik(YOO • pik) — Eskimo people who live on the western and southwestern coasts of Alaska and speak the Yupik language.

INDEX

About the Author

Alice Osinski has had a varied career in the field of education. She has been teacher consultant, director of bicultural curriculum and alternative education programs for Native American children, and producer of educational filmstrips. Ms. Osinski has written several articles about the unique life-style of Native Americans and has coauthored a filmstrip entitled Grandmother White Loon Feather's Thanksgiving. *She has written another book in the New True Book Series entitled* The Sioux.